Wind of a Thousand Tales

Folktale by
JOHN GLORE

With optional music
and lyrics by
DIANE KING

(Commissioned and originally produced by South Coast Repertory)

Family Plays

311 Washington St., Woodstock, IL 60098-3308
Phone: (800) 448-7469 / (815) 338-7170 • Fax: (800) 334-5302 / (815) 338-8981
www.FamilyPlays.com

*** NOTICE ***

The amateur and stock acting rights to this work are controlled exclusively by FAMILY PLAYS without whose permission in writing no performance of it may be given. Royalty must be paid every time a play is performed whether or not it is presented for profit and whether or not admission is charged. A play is performed any time it is acted before an audience. Current royalty rates, applications and restrictions may be found at our website **www.FamilyPlays.com**, or we may be contacted by mail at: FAMILY PLAYS, 311 Washington St., Woodstock IL 60098.

COPYRIGHT LAW GIVES THE AUTHOR OR THE AUTHOR'S AGENT THE EXCLUSIVE RIGHT TO MAKE COPIES. This law provides authors with a fair return for their creative efforts. Authors earn their living from the royalties they receive from book sales and from the performance of their work. Conscientious observance of copyright law is not only ethical it encourages authors to continue their creative work. This work is fully protected by copyright. No alterations, deletions or substitutions may be made in the work without the prior written consent of the publisher. No part of this work may be reproduced or transmitted in any form or by any means, electronic or mechanical, including photocopy, recording, videotape, film, or any information storage and retrieval system, without permission in writing from the publisher. It may not be performed either by professionals or amateurs without payment of royalty. All rights, including, but not limited to, the professional, motion picture, radio, television, videotape, foreign language, tabloid, recitation, lecturing, publication and reading, are reserved. *In all programs this notice must appear:*

"Produced by special arrangement with
FAMILY PLAYS of Woodstock, Illinois"

For performance of any songs, music and recordings mentioned in this play which are in copyright, the permission of the copyright owners must be obtained or other songs and recordings in the public domain substituted.

© 1991 by JOHN GLORE and DIANE KING

Printed in the United States of America
All Rights Reserved

(WIND OF A THOUSAND TALES)

ISBN: 978-0-88680-350-6

WIND OF A THOUSAND TALES

Cast

The Real People:
  Kimberly-Kay
  Her Mother
  Old Woman
    (Gramma Kim-Kay)
  Child One
  Child Two

The Breezes:
  Brisa
  Nushi
  Bluster

The Story People:
  I. Pepe
      María
      Juan
      Juanita
      Carlos
      Corazón
      Girl
      American Girl

      José
      Townspeople
  II. Kikushyo
      His Mother
      Kiyomi
      The Spirit
      Villagers
  III. Princess Anna
      Janos the Peasant
      His Mother
      The King
      Prince One ⎫
      Prince Two ⎬ same actor
      Prince Three ⎭
      Harold the Herald
      The Executioner
      Woman One ⎫ same
      Woman Two ⎭ actress
      Innkeeper
      Innkeeper's Daughter
      Townspeople

(An ensemble of 12 actors can play all the roles)

Δ

Kimberly-Kay's bedroom, today

Part I: A tale from Mexico
Part II: A tale from Japan
Part III: A tale from middle Europe

• Δ •

Wind of a Thousand Tales was originally produced in Costa Mesa, Calif., by South Coast Repertory's Young Conservatory Players, April 9-17, 1988, directed by Jose Cruz Gonzalez, with choreography by Molly Lynch, sets and costumes by Dwight Richard Odle, and lights by Donna Ruzika. Young Conservatory Players producer was Diane Doyle, and SCR artistic directors were David Emmes and Martin Benson. Original cast as follows:

Voice	Kris Hagen
Kimberly-Kay	Nicole Parker
Her Mother	Maureen Brophy
Brisa	Megan Mygatt
Pepe	Brian Simon
María	Beth Lockie
Juan	Michael Miller
Juanita	Maureen Brophy
Carlos	Paul Constantine
Corazón	Crissy Guerrero
American Girl	Darci Price
José	Stuart Gripman
Nushi	Michael Miller
Kikushyo	Robb Sasine
His Mother	Maureen Brophy
Kiyomi	Beth Lockie
The Spirit	Brian Simon
Musician	Stuart Gripman
Bluster	Paul Constantine
Princess Anna	Darci Price
Peasant Janos	Stuart Gripman
Janos's Mother	Megan Mygatt
The King	Brian Simon
Princes 1, 2, and 3	Michael Miller
Harold the Herald	Robb Sasine
The Executioner	Maureen Brophy
Woman 1, Woman 2	Crissy Guerrero
Innkeeper	Megan Mygatt
Innkeeper's Daughter	Beth Lockie
Gramma Kim-Kay	Kris Hagen
Child 1	Robb Sasine
Child 2	Megan Mygatt

ABOUT THE PLAY

Kimberly-Kay doesn't believe in make-believe. She is a child of tomorrow—a practical, matter-of-fact, no-nonsense kid, too grown up to listen to fairy tales, too sophisticated to have a happy childhood. And so, when her mother comes to tuck her in and tell her a bedtime story, Kimberly-Kay scoffs, turns over, and goes to sleep.

That's when the Wind of a Thousand Tales decides it's time to blow in and take charge. The Wind is made up of Breezes (played by an Ensemble of 8-34 or more actors) who have picked up countless folk tales on their travels around the world. In an effort to change Kimberly-Kay's attitude, the Breezes tell their stories—one from Mexico, one from Japan, and one from a middle-European country called Austro-slash-Hungaro-slash-Italo-hyphen-Beederburg.

By the time she has heard the three tales, Kimberly-Kay understands a deeper sense of truth than she had found in a world without make-believe.

Wind of a Thousand Tales received its world premiere at the South Coast Repertory in Costa Mesa, California, followed by productions by ChildsPlay in Tempe, Arizona; the California Theatre Center in Sunnyvale, and Vines High School in Plano, Texas. It is recommended for audiences of children from kindergarten through high school, but is enjoyable by adults, too. Playing time is 65-70 minutes, depending on whether or not music is used.

Wind of a Thousand Tales includes original songs and incidental music by South Coast Repertory composer Diane King. A conductor's score and a demo/accompaniment tape of the music are available from **Family Plays**. The songs may be omitted for a non-musical production. (See additional suggestions regarding music on p. 39.)

•

Critical Comments

"A dreamy, breezy illusion ... The magic is a concoction of John Glore's well written script ... The mood [of the Hispanic story] is created by Diane King's splendid Spanish ballad ... By the time Kimberly-Kay is plopped back into her bed, she has a healthy respect for stories ... and we're glad to have experienced her transformation. The added bonus is a good dose of (world) culture—a good enough reason to engage the whole family."—Marjorie Stradinger, *Irvine* (Calif.) *World News*

"Young audiences grow up to be adult audiences, and a good theatre-going habit cannot but help the quality and popularity of both amateur and professional regional theatre. The South Coast Repertory Theatre evidently thinks so because their children's theatre is celebrating the tenth anniversary with *Wind of a Thousand Tales* . . . a clever and absorbing story that combines three folk tales . . . The place was packed with youngsters from 4 and 5 on up . . . The three tales told to convince Kimberly-Kay that creative imagination is as important as any number of facts, are funny, poignant and important lessons for young people growing up, just the things that make Children's Theatre helpful for parents who want their children to learn from as well as enjoy experiencing the arts."—Robert S. Telford, *Long Beach* (Calif.) *News*

"The players, not the sets and costumes are the show . . .Kimberly-Kay . . . has no time for bedtime stories. Her mother . . . doesn't want her to be in such a hurry to grow up. One night, Kimberly-Kay is suddenly swept away by 'Winds of a Thousand Tales,' who bring her the magic of make-believe, acting out Mexican, Japanese, and European folk tales . . . Jose Cruz Gonzalez directs this refreshing hour; Diane King wrote the fine score . . . During the Japanese tale, Kimberly-Kay objects that the story isn't true. One of the winds replies, 'If it makes you feel something, then it has truth.' This production makes itself felt."—Lynne Heffley, *Los Angeles Times*

"In an age when computers create cartoons and TV commercials serve as the basis for children's TV shows, it might be a little rough for kids to really appreciate the magic of a good story. That's the premise of 'Wind of a Thousand Tales,' an upbeat, clever production . . . The show is billed as primarily a children's production, but adults can certainly enjoy its pleasant songs, tongue-in-cheek humor and some enchanting performances."—Greg Klerkx, *Orange Coast Daily Pilot*

"This play gave us much joy and satisfaction. It allowed the students to be creative and use acting skills that we had talked about in class. Our audiences, comprised of all ages from grandparents to very young children, were mesmerized by the story as well as the characters."
—Carla Ford, director, Vines High School, Plano, Texas

"Playable by adults or children . . . The original production effectively used only a bare stage with a few props . . . Costumes were suggested rather than realistically detailed . . . Intended audience: Ages

6-14; adults also enjoyed the show . . . The show is both simple and highly theatrical, encouraging the imaginative collaboration of its audiences to create the different worlds of the play . . . The play has important messages for children, but avoids teaching or preaching. It's a lot of fun."—ASSITEJ/USA "Best Available Plays" Project

WIND OF A THOUSAND TALES
PART I

[A VOICE comes out of blackness]

OLD WOMAN'S VOICE. Listen! *[Silence. Then the first faint sounds of WIND-MUSIC, created by the ENSEMBLE with whispers and hums]* Do you hear it? There is a wind—a warm, whispering, murmuring wind—a *magic* wind, made of all the voices that ever told a tale. Listen! A thousand voices of a thousand years, breathing stories into the ears of children, a Wind of a Thousand Tales, blowing round the world in the dark of night. Listen!

[LIGHTS dimly up on ENSEMBLE as the wind. They use billowing cloth to suggest the blowing wind]

Music #1: ONCE UPON A TIME

ENSEMBLE VOICES. *[Whispering, murmuring, building, and overlapping:]*
—Once upon a time . . .
—happily ever after . . .
—a handsome prince . . .
—into the woods . . .
—a kindly old woman . . .
—at the bottom of the sea . . .
—the frightening ogre . . .
—over the mountain . . .
—in a dark and dreary castle . . .
—the most beautiful . . .
—ugly witch . . .
—in the village . . .
—in the valley . . .
—clever . . .
—powerful . . .
—graceful . . .
—good-hearted . . .
—beastliest . . .
—of them all . . .

—happened once . . .
—once upon a time on top of a . . .
—once upon a time beside the . . .

[The whispering now turns into a SONG, sung by the ENSEMBLE:]

Once upon a time lived a princess,
Once upon a time was a fable told
'Bout a man and his son,
And the daughter of Juan,
And the beautiful dancer, Kiyomi.

Stories of love, stories of courage,
Journeys in darkness, travels in light,
Humor and wisdom, music and mirth . . .
This is the Wind of a Thousand Tales.
This is the Wind of a Thousand Tales.

GROUP I.	GROUP II.
Once upon a time	Once upon a time
In a town called Luzamor	Lived the dancer of the silver birds,
Lived a boy and . . .	And once,
Once upon a time	Once upon a time
Lived a princess with everything but—	Lived a princess with everything but—
True enough—	Only once—
Time it was—upon—	Upon once—
Once upon a time—	Once upon a, once upon a time—
Once . . .	Once upon a time . . .
Upon a time.	Once upon a time.

[As the MUSIC ends, the ENSEMBLE whispers again as they retire to the periphery of the stage:]

—Once upon a time . . .
  —upon a time . . .
    —once upon a time . . .
      —once upon a time . . .

OLD WOMAN'S VOICE. And then there is a girl, named Kimberly-Kay.

[Center Stage, under an oversized bedspread, a lump begins moving around frenetically. We hear KIMBERLY-KAY's voice:]

KIMBERLY-KAY. *[Petulantly]* I can't find my encyclopedia!
OLD WOMAN'S VOICE. And Kimberly-Kay hates stories.

[LIGHTS full up as KIMBERLY-KAY emerges from under the bedspread. She is a little child in a long flannel nightgown]

KIMBERLY-KAY. *[To audience]* I have to find my encyclopedia because if I don't, my mother is going to try to read me a bedtime story. And I hate stories. They're dumb. And they're boring. And most of them are totally untrue. *[Confidentially]* People just make them up. Our *own parents* make them up. And then they tell the stories to us kids to confuse us. But the truth is, the things in stories mostly never happened. I mean, Goldilocks was never a real person. And who here has actually *seen* a fairy godmother? Or a *bean*stalk? They're all just big fat fibs, and me, I'd rather know true things. I've tried to explain this to my mother, but she still comes in here every night and wants to read me a bedtime story. Watch: five, four, three, two, one— *[She points off, and her MOTHER enters, right on cue]*

MOTHER. Ready for bed, pumpkin? I'll tuck you in and then why don't I read you the story of Little Red Riding Hood?

KIMBERLY-KAY. *[As she continues talking to us, she gets into bed. The bed is the pile of fabric]* See? Mother. Let me tell *you* the story of Little Red Riding Hood. A ditzy little girl goes into a dangerous forest wearing bright red—talk about asking for trouble—then she stops in the middle of the forest to have a conversation with a wolf—oh really?—and the wolf asks where Little Red is going and she *tells* him. And then she's surprised when the wolf tries to eat her and her gramma. What is the *point* here? If you have to read to me, why don't you help me find my encyclopedia and start reading the C's.

MOTHER. Something's not right with you, Kimberly-Kay. All little children are supposed to like stories.

KIMBERLY-KAY. I'm a child of tomorrow, Mother. We don't have time for make-believe.

Music #2: CHILD OF TOMORROW

KIMBERLY-KAY. *[Sings:]* Why should I listen to fairy tales?
    That's not reality!
    Why should I ponder on dreams and disaster
    When none of it matters to me?

MOTHER. *[Sings:]* Kimberly-Kay,
    You can learn a lot from fairy tales.
    Not everything in the world
    Is math and science, honest!
    Living in day dreams,
    Using your mind to create,
    And imagining other worlds
    Is fine.

KIMBERLY-KAY. That's not factual, true or practical!
    What's the point?
    I like history; those are stories
    That make sense to me.
    Come on, Mother, it's no big deal,
    But make-believe? Be real!
    Black or white, true or false,
    I want it straight
    'Cause I'm a child of tomorrow.
    Here and now, right or wrong,
    I know my fate
    'Cause I'm a child of tomorrow.
    No illusions, no magic trips,
    No dilemmas and no despair.
    Information to the max,
    Only time for cold hard facts!

KIMBERLY-KAY.	MOTHER.
Black or white, true or false,	Brightness and
I want it straight	Color.
'Cause I'm a child of tomorrow.	
Here and now, right or wrong,	Shadow and
I know my fate	Light.
'Cause I'm a child of tomorrow.	

    MOTHER. Don't be so serious,
        There's plenty of time to grow up.

Loosen up a little,
Come on, dream a little,
Reach for something above.
Just let go, and try some make-believe!
KIMBERLY-KAY. Black or white, true or false,
   I want it straight
   'Cause I'm a child of tomorrow.
   Here and now, right or wrong,
   I know my fate
   'Cause I'm a child of tomorrow.

KIMBERLY-KAY.	MOTHER.
Black or white, true or false,	We can argue all night about
I want it straight	Make-believe.
'Cause I'm a child of tomorrow.	
Here and now, right or wrong,	Trust me, I know I'm right
I know my fate	And some day you'll see.
'Cause I'm a child of tomorrow.	
Black or white,	Some day,
True or false,	Soon.
I want it straight	
'Cause I'm a child of tomorrow.	
Child of tomorrow!	

MOTHER. *[Frustrated]* Some day, Kimberly-Kay Copernicus— Oh, never mind. Good night. Sleep tight. Don't let the bedbugs bite.

KIMBERLY-KAY. There's no such thing as bedbugs, Mother. G'night.

[LIGHTS go out, except for moonlight shining through a window on Kimberly-Kay. Two people holding billowing fabric can form the window. Very faintly, the WIND-MUSIC returns. KIMBERLY-KAY pulls the covers up tightly around her]

KIMBERLY-KAY. She means well. But she's trapped in the olden days. Kids don't need bedtime stories any more. The other day I was telling my friend, Crayola— *[A sudden gust of "WIND"—embodied by one of the Ensemble—blows through the bedroom, cutting Kimberly-Kay off in mid-sentence]* Gee, it's kind of spooky out tonight. The way the moon is shining through my window. And I've never heard the wind blow like that before. Anyway— *[WIND-MUSIC grows louder. Then another "BREEZE," played by one of the Ensemble with a bil-*

lowing cloth, blows through the bedroom. This time KIMBERLY-KAY sees it] What the—Did you see that? [Another "BREEZE" blows through, then TWO more] This is really peculiar.

[The WIND-MUSIC becomes quite loud and the ENSEMBLE, as the wind, converges on Kimberly-Kay's bed, swirling around it, "blowing" her hair, etc. Then they lift the bed with her on it and carry her around the stage, whisper-singing "Kimberly-Kay, Blow her away, Kimberly-Kay, Blow her away." KIMBERLY-KAY buries herself in the covers]

KIMBERLY-KAY. Yikes!

OLD WOMAN'S VOICE. Kimberly-Kay was beginning to realize that this was no ordinary wind. It was the Wind of a Thousand Tales, and now it carried Kimberly-Kay right out her bedroom window and high into the night sky, above the clouds, higher and higher.

[KIMBERLY-KAY tentatively peeks out from under the covers, then sits up, astonished. A BIRD-PUPPET flies across the stage and is shocked to see Kimberly-Kay fly by in the opposite direction. A few other things fly by: a sheet of newspaper, an umbrella, etc.]

KIMBERLY-KAY. This can't be happening to me. I don't live in some fairy tale where little girls get lifted up into the sky in the middle of the night. Put me down! Woooooa!

OLD WOMAN'S VOICE. Below her, Kimberly-Kay could see the countryside flashing by, faster than a dream. And then, when she began to think she might never feel the earth beneath her feet again, the wind took her ever so gently to the ground, setting her down in a dark and mysterious forest.

[The ENSEMBLE sets her down and the LIGHTS dim to black]

KIMBERLY-KAY. [In darkness] Hey! I can't see! Good thing I brought Sparky.

[Suddenly a FLASHLIGHT—Sparky—comes on. The beam searches the area, and as it does, MOONLIGHT comes up slowly to reveal a forest of TREES played by the Ensemble. They continue softly vocalizing the sound of the wind, and their branches *wave gently in the breeze. KIMBERLY-KAY has a look-around with Sparky]*

KIMBERLY-KAY. Where the heck am I? *[She wanders among the human Trees]* I don't like the looks of these trees. *[The "WIND" gusts, momentarily, causing all the TREES to bend suddenly toward KIMBERLY-KAY, who scurries back to her bed]* Maybe I'm dreaming. Yeah! That's it. This is just a dream! *[From one of the Trees comes the voice of BRISA]*

BRISA. It's no dream.

KIMBERLY-KAY. *[Whirling around]* Who said that?

BRISA. I did.

KIMBERLY-KAY. *[Scratching her head]* I could have sworn that voice came from one of these trees.

BRISA. *[Stepping forward]* It did. Hello, Kimberly-Kay. Welcome to Nowhere.

KIMBERLY-KAY. *[Rubbing her eyes]* This can't be happening.

BRISA. *[Laughing]* Of course it can. Anything can happen in Nowhere.

KIMBERLY-KAY. Nowhere?

BRISA. Nowhere!

KIMBERLY-KAY. Wait a minute! There's no such place as Nowhere. Show it to me on a map.

BRISA. *[Finding the idea quite amusing]* I can't show you Nowhere on a map! Nowhere is a secret place. Nowhere is the home of the Wind of a Thousand Tales.

KIMBERLY-KAY. Is that so? And who are you? Tinker Bell?

BRISA. *[Curtseying]* I am Brisa—a little breeze from Mexico.

KIMBERLY-KAY. A breeze. Right. As in— *[KIMBERLY-KAY puffs up her cheeks and blows]*

BRISA. *[Clapping, enjoying the display]* That's right!

KIMBERLY-KAY. If you're a breeze, how come I can see you?

BRISA. Because when I'm at home in Nowhere, I can look like anything I want. A moment ago I was a tree. Now I'm a *beautiful* lady. *[With a tinge of sarcasm]* But if you'd rather, I could become a tractor. Or an overhead projector.

KIMBERLY-KAY. Well look, Brisa, it's really great that you're a breeze and everything, but I'm a little girl, and I don't belong in Nowhere, I don't even believe in Nowhere, so I'm just going to close my eyes and when I open them again I expect to be back in my bedroom, okay? *[She closes her eyes tightly, then opens them. BRISA smiles]*

BRISA. I'm sorry, Kimberly-Kay, but you can't go back yet. We brought you here for a reason.

KIMBERLY-KAY. We? Who's "we"?

BRISA. *[Indicating the trees]* The other breezes and I. Together we make up the Wind of a Thousand Tales, and we spirited you away from your bedroom tonight because we've heard that you don't like stories.

KIMBERLY-KAY. Yeah? So?

BRISA. Well, without stories we wouldn't exist. And if other children follow your example and stop wanting stories, the Wind of a Thousand Tales will soon die out forever; and all of us breezes will die too.

KIMBERLY-KAY. So what are you going to do to me?

BRISA. Slow torture. *[A burst of giggling from the TREES]* I'm joking, sourpuss. All we're going to do is tell you three of our stories. If we can convince you that stories are a good thing, then we will happily take you back to your bedroom.

KIMBERLY-KAY. What if you can't?

BRISA. Then the Wind of a Thousand Tales will stop blowing forever—and you'll have to find your own way home. Now sit. The first story is mine, and since I am a Mexicana breeze, I will tell you a story from Mexico.

KIMBERLY-KAY. Listen, this is a big waste of time. Read my lips: I don't like stories.

THE BREEZES. *[Blowing and bending all together]* Sssssssssssit!

KIMBERLY-KAY. Right! *[She quickly sits]*

BRISA. That's much better. And now, the tale of Carlos and Corazón.

[LIGHTS dim. KIMBERLY-KAY, BRISA, and the ENSEMBLE not involved in the story move out of the main playing area. **Music #3: Guitar Underscore.** *In darkness we hear:]*

BRISA. Once upon a time in the very heart of Mexico there was a little town called Luzamor. Luzamor was a happy place, full of light and love. Now there lived in Luzamor two wealthy men and their lovely wives, who were the best of friends. *[LIGHTS up on the four]* One day María said to her husband—

MARIA. Pepe, I'm going to have a niño!

BRISA'S VOICE. There was much celebration— *[The FOUR jump up and down and hug one another]* And then Pepe said to his friends, Juan and Juanita—
PEPE. Juan. Juanita. You will be the baby's godparents! *[More jumping and hugging]*
BRISA'S VOICE. At the end of the year the little one was born, a beautiful niño, and they named him— *[LIGHTS up on handsome kid]*
CARLOS. *[Proudly]* Carlos.

[The PARENTS and GODPARENTS gather around Carlos and fawn over him, saying his name in adoring baby talk]

BRISA'S VOICE. Then, two years later, Juan and Juanita had their own child, a little girl they named— *[SPOTLIGHT up on Corazón]*
CORAZON. Corazón.

[The OTHERS, who had continued their bubbly celebration, fall silent and turn to look at Corazón, wave halfheartedly, then go back to doting on Carlos]

BRISA'S VOICE. Carlos and Corazón grew up together and they were very close, like brother and sister. *[CARLOS and CORAZON play together as little children, the four PARENTS looking on]*
CARLOS. Let's play Palace. I will be the handsome prince, and you can be—
CORAZON. The princess?
CARLOS. No, you can be the old nurse who takes care of my every need!
CORAZON. *[Only a little disappointed]* Oh. All right.
BRISA'S VOICE. That's how most of their games went. Then, one day, Corazón's parents died— *[LIGHT on her PARENTS fades, and they move to the periphery of the stage]* Everyone was very sad, but Pepe said—
PEPE. Don't worry, Corazón. You may come and live with us.
BRISA'S VOICE. And so Corazón became a part of Carlos's family, and she and Carlos became closer still. Corazón grew into a gentle, good-hearted young lady, who loved music more than anything. *[CORAZON reads a book and hums a sweet melody]* Carlos, on the other hand, grew into a very handsome, but very vain and frivolous young man. When he should have been thinking about his heart and his mind and his soul, he thought only of his well-combed hair. He flirted

with all the girls in the town, and by the time he was sixteen he had broken many hearts— *[A GIRL approaches him, gives him a Valentine, which he cheerfully tears in half. She runs off crying]* —and after each broken heart he would say to Corazón—

CARLOS. She was not beautiful enough for me. I would rather be blind than marry an ugly girl.

BRISA'S VOICE. Now the truth was, Corazón loved Carlos very much, but she believed she was not a beautiful girl, so she could only turn her face downward and say—

CORAZON. Yes, Carlos. And the girl you marry must be good-hearted as well as beautiful.

CARLOS. *[Baffled]* Good-hearted?

KIMBERLY-KAY. Hold it!

[At this point the ACTION FREEZES and KIMBERLY-KAY walks into the story. She checks out Carlos and Corazón, poking them to see if they're real, as she says:]

KIMBERLY-KAY. Excuse me, Brisa, this is a great story and all, but if I don't get home soon my mother's going to ground me for—

BRISA. You are a rude little girl. Now get out of my story and let me finish it.

KIMBERLY-KAY. *[Returning to her place]* Okay! Why couldn't I have been carried away by the wind of a thousand encyclopedias?

[The story's ACTION RESUMES]

BRISA'S VOICE. One day a beautiful American girl came to Luzamor to buy some authentic Mexican combs for her hair. When Carlos saw her—

CARLOS. Caramba, qué linda!

BRISA'S VOICE. —he thought she was the most beautiful girl in the world.

CARLOS. This is the chiquita for me! What's your name, señorita?

AMERICAN GIRL. *[Very conceited]* Mary Elizabeth Bancroft-Jones. But you may call me Poopsie.

CARLOS. Poopsie, Poopsie, Poopsie! *[He grabs her hand and does a little dance, literally sweeping her off her feet]*

BRISA'S VOICE. Carlos introduced the American girl to his parents and announced that he wished to marry her.

PEPE and MARIA. *[Less than enthusiastic]* Wonderful news, mijo.

BRISA'S VOICE. But his parents were not very happy. You see, they wanted him to marry Corazón, for they knew that she loved him very much. But they always let Carlos have what he wanted, so they made preparations for a great engagement celebration. On the evening of the fiesta, their home was filled with laughter— *[Music #4A. ENSEMBLE enters, filling the stage with laughter]* and dancing— *[Music #4B. ENSEMBLE members pair off and dance]* —but when it came time to be entertained with song, the singers were nowhere to be found. They had all gotten drunk and fallen into the lake. Carlos's father was very upset—

PEPE. *[To Brisa]* What do you mean they fell into the lake! We have to have singers or I'll be the laughing-stock of the town! *[BRISA shrugs. CORAZON comes forward]*

CORAZON. Tio Pepe, I will sing.

CARLOS. What?! *[Trying to pull her back]* No, no, no, Corazón. You can't do that. How would that look? You're part of the family. You can't demean yourself by entertaining our guests. Besides . . . you're not very pretty and . . . and you're wearing such a *plain* dress. You'd embarrass me by calling attention to yourself.

PEPE. Carlos, your tongue is like a happy, stupid dog, the way it wags. Still, Corazón, he's right that you shouldn't have to sing for the guests in your own home.

CORAZON. Tio Pepe. Please. Let me sing.

PEPE. *[After a pause]* Very well, my child.

BRISA'S VOICE. So as everyone stopped their laughing and dancing and turned to listen, Corazón opened her heart and sang.

Music #5: CORAZON

CORAZON. *[Sings:]*
(Chorus) Canción de mi corazón;
    Canto d'amor,
    Canto de paz,
    Canto de felicidad.

    Canción de mi corazón;
    Con alegria,
    Canto d'amor,
    Toda mi vida.

(Verse)
>Vuela mi corazón
>Como la paloma blanca,
>Libre de pena,
>Lleno de placer,
>Vuela! Vuela!

(Chorus)
(Verse)
>Y mi amor, cerca de mi,
>Me levante al cielo azul.
>Nos juntamos con las estrellas
>Y bailamos con los angelitos;
>Vuela! Vuela!

(Chorus)
(Coda)
>Cancion de mi corazón;
>Vuela! Vuela!

BRISA'S VOICE. When Corazón finished her song, all the guests seemed to disappear from Carlos's sight. *[They back away to the dark periphery of the stage. CARLOS looks at CORAZON, who stands with head bowed on the opposite side of the stage]* Carlos looked at Corazón as if he had never seen her before.

CARLOS. I have never heard such a beautiful voice in all my life. I don't understand, suddenly I feel . . . I feel . . . *[Approaching her]* Corazón! Corazón! Your song has enchanted me! I've decided that only you can be my wife. *[He smiles and opens his arms expectantly, but CORAZON doesn't move]*

CORAZON. Surely you mock me, Carlos. I have heard you say many times that you would rather be blind than marry an ugly girl. I know that I am not nearly pretty enough for you, so please don't make fun of me by asking me to be your wife. *[She turns and quickly exits]*

BRISA'S VOICE. Suddenly Carlos felt very unhappy. He'd never thought about his heart before, or he would understand that now it was breaking. For the next three months he tried desperately to make Corazón change her mind, but she knew that she would always be ugly in his eyes.

CARLOS. Please, Corazón! I'll let you comb my hair.

BRISA'S VOICE. But Corazón would not hear his pleas. Finally, no longer able to bear the pain in his heart, Carlos bade his parents a sad farewell—
PEPE. Adiós, mijo.
MARIA. Stay on the path, and don't talk to strangers.
BRISA'S VOICE. —and moved to another town, far away.

[The playing area is momentarily empty; then BRISA and KIMBERLY-KAY cross slowly to Center, watching CARLOS exit]

KIMBERLY-KAY. *[Momentarily caught up in the tale]* That's so sad... But kinda stupid. If he's in love with her and she's in love with him, then what's the big problem?
BRISA. I can see you know nothing about love.
KIMBERLY-KAY. Yeah-huh, I looked it up once. But... just out of curiosity... what happened to Carlos?

[BRISA smiles as she and K-K cross to the edge of the stage. CARLOS enters holding a candle and begins writing. Music #6]

BRISA'S VOICE. Several years passed. Although Carlos knew that his own stupidity had cost him Corazón's love, he could not forget her. He faithfully wrote a letter to her every night for a thousand nights. But he never mailed the letters because he feared Corazón would only throw them away. Worse yet, because he wrote so many letters by the dim light of a single candle, his eyes weakened until one day he found that he could no longer see. *[An ENSEMBLE member puts a black blindfold over Carlos's eyes]*
CARLOS. Can anyone be unhappier than I? I have lost my eyesight *and* the love of my dearest Corazón. What shall I do? *[Carlos's friend JOSE appears]*
JOSE. I'll tell you what to do, amigo—
BRISA'S VOICE. —said Carlos's friend, José.
JOSE. You need a woman to take care of you. Why don't you find yourself a nice—
CARLOS. No.
JOSE. —young—
CARLOS. No.
JOSE. —good-looking—
CARLOS. No!
JOSE. —nurse!

CARLOS. Oh. That's not a bad idea, José. I could use some help around here. But I don't know where to find a nurse.

JOSE. Leave that to me, hombre. *[JOSE crosses the stage to Corazón's area]*

CORAZON. You want me to be his nurse? It's true I love Carlos, but he doesn't love me. *[Thinking for a moment]* José, I will go to him, but only on one condition. You must promise never to tell him who I am. Since he cannot see me, my ugliness will no longer shame him, and I will work as his faithful nurse as long as he needs me.

BRISA'S VOICE. So Corazón went to Carlos and cared for him. She cooked for him, walked with him, read to him. And as time passed, Carlos grew very fond of his gentle nurse, never guessing that she was his own Corazón.

CARLOS. Nurse, you have been most kind to me. Now I'm going to share a secret with you. Under my bedding you'll find a bundle of letters. Take them out and bring them to me. *[She does]* These love letters cost me my eyes, but they were well worth that price. I wrote them for the woman who might have been my wife, if not for the blindness of my heart. Nurse, please: read to me the letters I wrote for the beautiful, good-hearted Corazón?

BRISA'S VOICE. And so Corazón read his letters, one by one. She read of his love, of his faith, of his sorrow. All night long she read, and when morning came she knew that Carlos truly loved her. For in his letters, she had seen his heart. *[Pause]* The next morning, that little matchmaker, José, decided to take matters into his own hands.

JOSE. *[Entering]* Carlos, perhaps Corazón has finally forgiven you. Wouldn't you like me to ask her, one last time, to be your wife?

CARLOS. José, if you can convince Corazón to marry me, I will give you half my fortune.

JOSE. I want half your fortune *and* . . . your combs.

CARLOS. My combs? José, take it from me, combs can lead to a lot of trouble. But you're welcome to them.

JOSE. Bueno! Wait here.

BRISA'S VOICE. So José went to Corazón, and she agreed without hesitation to give her heart to her beloved Carlos. When José brought her to Carlos—

[Music #7: Dressing Music. As BRISA speaks, JOSE leads CORAZON around the periphery of the stage as the marimba

music plays. *They interact with members of the ENSEMBLE, who dress Corazón in wedding regalia as she passes. Finally JOSE leads her back to Carlos and links her hands to his]*

CARLOS. Corazón, is it you? . . . Corazón? . . . Say something.

Music #8: CORAZON reprise

[CORAZON sings a few lines of the song she sang earlier, after which she and CARLOS embrace. KIMBERLY-KAY and BRISA move toward the couple]

CARLOS. *[Removing his blindfold]* And when Corazón told Carlos that all along she had been his faithful nurse—

CORAZON. —he wept for joy, for he saw as clearly as any man can see—

CARLOS. —that in this good-hearted woman he had found true beauty.

[KIMBERLY-KAY stares at them, enraptured. After a moment, she snaps out of it and turns to Brisa]

KIMBERLY-KAY. The end?
BRISA. The end. Did you like the story?
KIMBERLY-KAY. I guess it was okay. Kinda mushy.
BRISA. *[Disappointed]* I'm sorry it didn't please you more. It is time for me to go now. *[She steps backward with CARLOS and CORAZON into the shadows]* The next tale will not be so happy, so perhaps you will like it more. Good-bye, Kimberly-Kay. *[BRISA is gone]*
KIMBERLY-KAY. Wait! Brisa, come back. Don't be sad, I did kind of like your story . . . Brisa! *[The LIGHTS suddenly go to black, as though a cloud has passed in front of the moon]* Oh no, what happened to the moonlight? Help! Brisa! Anybody! Mommy? Where's Sparky?

[She finds the flashlight and turns it on. The LIGHTS slowly come back up, and now KIMBERLY-KAY finds herself in the middle of a field of very large MUSHROOMS]

PART II

KIMBERLY-KAY. Now what? Where'd all these humongous mushrooms come from?

[KIMBERLY-KAY is startled by the knocking of Kabuki CLACKERS and a brief, haunting strain on a Japanese flute (Music #9A)]

KIMBERLY-KAY. *[Sing-song]* I have a funny feeling about this. *[Suddenly, one of the "mushrooms" rises up to become NUSHI. The top of the mushroom is a Japanese straw hat]*
NUSHI. *[Cheerfully]* Hello, Kim-Kay.
KIMBERLY-KAY. Uh, hi. Don't tell me. You're a breeze, right?
NUSHI. *[Nodding]* I am Nushi. I blew in from Japan.
KIMBERLY-KAY. And you're here to tell me a tale.
NUSHI. Yes, I am a tale-wind. *[Short burst of laughter from the MUSHROOMS]* Little joke. Now, please to sit down and hear the story of the Silver-Bird Dancer.
KIMBERLY-KAY. *[As she and NUSHI withdraw to a corner]* Well, okay. But do you think you could make it quick? I have a short attention span.
NUSHI. The story will last exactly as long as it lasts.
KIMBERLY-KAY. That long, hunh?
NUSHI. *[With a little bow]* Hanashi aimoshita . . . This story happened in a long-ago time. It is the story of a boy who was finished being a boy, but hadn't yet discovered how to be a man. His name was Kikushyo. *[Music #9B. A mushroom rises to become KIKUSHYO]* He lived in a village of farmers. Like everyone else in his village, Kikushyo's life revolved around the planting and harvesting of rice.

[Suddenly the field of "mushrooms" comes to life. It is the VILLAGERS, planting a field of rice, joined by KIKUSHYO. They plant in a dance-like rhythm defined by a happy musical chant:]

Music #10: RICE SONG

WOMEN. Ho ho hoi!
MEN. Sun, moon, river, and rain,
WOMEN. Favor our fields with plenty rice again.
MEN. Hai! Hai!
WOMEN. River and rain and sun and moon.

MEN. Ho ho hoi!
WOMEN. Laughing and working together in the fields,
MEN. Under sun, under moon, in the silver falling rain!
WOMEN. Hai! Hai!
MEN. Happy are we in the world,
WOMEN. In the world!
ALL. Happy are we in the world!

[As the OTHERS freeze, KIKUSHYO separates himself from the group and draws pictures in the dirt with his finger]

NUSHI. But Kikushyo dreamed of a different life.
KIKUSHYO. Rice, rice, rice. My life is nothing but rice. How I long to travel to the Royal City and become a painter in the court of the great Shogun.
NUSHI. Then, one day— *[A WOMAN emerges from the riceplanters and approaches Kikushyo]*
KIKUSHYO. *[Caught shirking his duty]* Oh, hello, Mother, I was just—I mean—
MOTHER. 'Kushyo, here you are again, drawing in the dirt while the rice waits to be planted.
KIKUSHYO. I know, Mother, it's just that—
MOTHER. Rice is all we have to fill our stomachs, 'Kushyo.
KIKUSHYO. But it's plain and white and has no taste.
MOTHER. And you must have a life of many rich colors and flavors, I know. *[Considering him for a moment]* Some spirit must be calling you away. I only hope it is a good spirit. Here, take these coins—all that I have in the world—and go to the Royal City. When you have become a great painter, you will feed the world with beauty.
KIKUSHYO. But—
MOTHER. Go on. The rice will grow without you.
NUSHI. And so Kikushyo took leave of his mother and set out on the road to the Royal City of Edo, two days' journey away. *[KIKUSHYO begins walking and the ENSEMBLE retires to the periphery of the stage, beating a walking rhythm. His MOTHER shouts after him:]*
MOTHER. Stay on the path, and don't talk to strangers!
NUSHI. *[Music #10A: Rice Song Reprise (underscore)]* Kikushyo walked, totsu-totsu-totsu, up into the hills and then, dotsu-dotsu-dotsu, down into the valley, until finally, as he entered the great forest, the day was swallowed by twilight.

[LIGHTS dim. Perhaps the ENSEMBLE becomes the forest trees. They begin to create the music of twilight]

KIKUSHYO. It grows so dark. I must find a place to spend the night.

NUSHI. Kikushyo walked and walked, but he found no resting place. He thought of sleeping beneath a tree, but you know, Kim-Kay, in the forest the night can be a cold and frightening bedfellow. The wind seemed to sing of spirits and demons, and the night animals taunted Kikushyo with their hooting and howling. *[SOUND: wind, wolves, owls, monkeys. KIKUSHYO creeps fearfully onward]* Then Kikushyo's heart lept with joy. In the distance, off the path and far into the woods, he could see a single friendly light.

[SPECIAL very slowly rises on KIYOMI, her back to Kikushyo on the opposite side of the stage. She holds a candle]

KIKUSHYO. I know my mother said not to stray from the path, but perhaps that light will lead me to a resting place for the night, away from all these terrible noises.

NUSHI. So Kikushyo made his way toward the light . . . and found that it came from the window of a very small cottage. He knocked upon the cottage door, don-a-don, and was surprised when the door opened to reveal— *[KIYOMI turns to face him]*

KIKUSHYO. *[Out to the audience]* —A beautiful lady! *[To Kiyomi]* Excuse me for intruding, gentle maiden, but I am on a journey to the Royal City and have no place to rest my head for the night. Do you have a corner where I may sleep? I will gladly pay you whatever— *[With a motion of her hand KIYOMI silences him, then beckons him to enter. She remains expressionless but has a haunted, mysterious quality, a little bit creepy. She moves with dancelike grace]*

NUSHI. The woman kept a dark silence, and as she prepared a meal for Kikushyo, he wondered who she was and why she lived alone in the forest.

KIKUSHYO. She can't be a peasant woman—her hands are so soft, and her face so pretty. And look how she moves, like a dancer. If only she would talk so I could hear the sound of her voice. *[She brings him his meal, then, in a sad, quiet voice, she speaks:]*

KIYOMI. Here is some food. I haven't much to offer. I seldom receive visitors.

KIKUSHYO. *[Mesmerized]* Thank you. *[KIYOMI kneels across from him, at a discreet distance, as KIKUSHYO eats his meal with chopsticks]* My name is Kikushyo. What's yours?
KIYOMI. *[All her answers are hesitant]* I am Kiyomi.
KIKUSHYO. Kiyomi. A pretty name. Have you always lived in the forest, Kiyomi-san?
KIYOMI. No.
KIKUSHYO. Oh... Where did you live before?
KIYOMI. In my True Love's heart.
KIKUSHYO. I see. Is that far from here?
KIYOMI. Very far.
KIKUSHYO. And do you have no family? Why do you live alone?
[Silence]
KIYOMI. While you finish your meal, I will prepare a place for you to sleep. The hour is late, and your journey is long. *[She begins laying out a futon]* I hope the futon will not be too hard for you. *[She places a screen next to the futon. TWO actors holding translucent cloth could form the screen]*
KIKUSHYO. Oh, that reminds me of a joke my friend, Akira, told me. There was this fat samurai who—
KIYOMI. You will sleep now.
KIKUSHYO. Oh. I thought perhaps we could stay up and talk for a while longer?
KIYOMI. You will sleep now... and... whatever you might hear in the night, do not move from behind the screen.
KIKUSHYO. All right. Good night, Kiyomi-san. May your dreams be happy. *[He smiles warmly]*
KIYOMI. Good night... Sleep well. *[A faint, sad smile briefly lightens her face. She blows out one or two candles and then kneels, head bowed and back to Kikushyo, some distance away on the other side of the screen. LIGHTS completely down except for faint moonlight on Kikushyo]*
NUSHI. But Kikushyo could not sleep. Outside the wind blew its ghostly song, gaya-gaya— *[ENSEMBLE creates sound of wind]* —and as Kikushyo tossed and turned in the night, he could not stop thinking about Kiyomi. *[KIKUSHYO's thoughts are whispered by three ENSEMBLE members, who swirl around him as Kikushyo tosses and turns:]*
ENSEMBLE. Who could she be? Why is she so silent and sad?

What did she mean about her True Love's heart? Who could she be? Who could she be? Who could she be? Why is she so silent and sad? What did she mean about her True Love's heart? Who could she be? Who could she be? Who could she be?

NUSHI. —Then!—came the hour of the rat, the deepest and darkest hour of the night. Kikushyo was startled from his thoughts by a frightening sound. *[Kabuki CLACKERS]* A cold chill went down his spine, jimi-jimi, and then, as though the wind itself were singing, Kikushyo heard a strange and beautiful music.

Music #11: KIYOMI'S DANCE

[As the dance music begins, KIKUSHYO sits up to listen. He cocks his ear, and the song seems to pull him closer and closer to the edge of the screen, which seems to sway to the music. NUSHI speaks over the song]

NUSHI. Kikushyo remembered Kiyomi's warning not to move from behind the screen, but the song seemed to pull him from his bed.
KIKUSHYO. I have to see. *[He peers cautiously under or around the screen]*
NUSHI. Although it was very dark, Kikushyo's straining eyes could make out a shadow moving in time with the eery music. *[The moonlight gradually increases to illuminate KIYOMI's dance. She wears a special kimono with distinct markings—silver birds]*
KIKUSHYO. It's Kiyomi!

[The dance begins quietly with very small, slow movements, but it gradually becomes more and more intense. Perhaps the dance involves fans, or cloth, or streamers. As the dance reaches its climax, KIYOMI makes a bold move toward KIKUSHYO, causing him to gasp, at which point the dance and the MUSIC come to a sudden halt. KIYOMI freezes in mid-movement. After a moment, to the sound of Kabuki CLACKERS, she turns her head with stylized movement, and her gaze locks on the trembling KIKUSHYO. She seems possessed. She moves toward him, slowly, inexorably, a wild look in her eyes. He is frozen in fear. She produces an ornate knife from the folds of her costume, and unsheathes it. She raises it high above her head, and just as she is about to bring it down upon KIKUSHYO, he and KIMBERLY-KAY cry out:]

KIKUSHYO and KIMBERLY-KAY. No! *[KIYOMI stops, slowly comes out of her demonic trance. She crumples to the ground like a wilting flower. After a long silence:]*

KIYOMI. *[Quietly]* You were told to stay behind the screen. Is this how you repay my kindness?

KIKUSHYO. *[Ashamed]* Forgive me, Kiyomi-san, but your dance entranced me. I could not stop myself from looking. *[After a moment, KIYOMI looks up at Kikushyo. Her face softens]*

KIYOMI. It is I who should ask your forgiveness. You are my guest, and I have treated you very badly. Come, sit by the fire, and I will tell you the meaning of my dancing.

NUSHI. And so, as the fire crackled, kachi-kachi, she told him her story.

[Perhaps KIMBERLY-KAY and NUSHI join KIKUSHYO and KIYOMI at her fire—as long as it's clear they're in two different realities. (Music #11A may be heard)]

KIYOMI. Do you know what a shirabyoshi is?

KIKUSHYO. A shirabyoshi is a great dancer.

KIYOMI. Three years ago I was a shirabyoshi, the finest in Kyoto. I was invited to dance before all the highest nobles. Because I always wore this special kimono, I was called the Silver-Bird Dancer.

KIKUSHYO. I've heard that name, even in my distant village!

KIYOMI. There was a young man, the son of the Shogun, destined to become the ruler of the land.

[LIGHTS dimly up on the SPIRIT, on the other side of the stage. Perhaps he holds up some translucent material through which we see his face. Or the fabric is draped over his head, ghost-like]

KIYOMI. You see his picture, there. *[She points in the direction of the SPIRIT. He may remain motionless, or he might enact in mime some of the story she tells]* He came to see my performances every night, and the beauty of my dancing and singing caused him to fall in love with me. He was noble, intelligent, and kind, and I grew to love him as he loved me.

KIKUSHYO. Did you marry him?

KIYOMI. Impossible. His father would never have allowed such a marriage.

KIKUSHYO. So what did you do?

KIYOMI. I swore my undying love to him, but for his sake I refused to become his wife. This upset him greatly so that he began to neglect his duties and to forget the respect owed to his royal father. I feared for him and could think of only one way to stop him from destroying himself. So one night . . . *[She weeps quietly, then collects herself]*

KIKUSHYO. *[Comforting her]* You don't have to tell me any more—

KIYOMI. One night, as the city slept, I crept away from my home, taking only this kimono and enough money to buy my food. I came to this place, far, far away from him, so that he would forget me. I never saw him again.

KIKUSHYO. And did he become the Shogun?

KIYOMI. When he discovered my disappearance, he only grew more distressed. He searched the kingdom for many months, without sleeping or eating, until finally he grew too weak to go on. He returned to his father's palace . . . and after a terrible sickness . . . he changed his world. All this I learned much later, from a passing stranger.

KIKUSHYO. Changed his world? You mean . . . he died?

KIYOMI. *[Nodding]* Now, although I can never see him again, I have sworn to dance for his spirit every night in the kimono he loved. That is why I urged you to sleep and asked you not to come out from behind the screen no matter what you heard. My dance is for his spirit alone.

[The LIGHT fades on the Spirit. Silence. If KIMBERLY-KAY and NUSHI joined Kiyomi and Kikushyo earlier, they now separate from them]

NUSHI. Kikushyo felt great pity for Kiyomi. They remained silent for the rest of the night while only the fire whispered, kachi-kachi. The next morning:

KIKUSHYO. Please let me pay you for your kindness.

KIYOMI. No. The only payment I ask is that you never tell anyone of me, and that you never repeat my story while I am of this world.

KIKUSHYO. I promise.

NUSHI. And Kikushyo kept his promise.

KIMBERLY-KAY. What happened to them?

[As NUSHI continues, a member of the ENSEMBLE uses his finger to apply a few simple lines of make-up to Kikushyo's face—under his eyes, at the corners of his mouth, on his forehead, to denote age]

NUSHI. Kikushyo went on to Edo and, as the years passed, he became a famous artist. Old age painted lines upon his face while his own brushes painted beauty in the court of the Shogun. He acquired great wealth and honor. One day, an old woman came to him. *[KIYOMI, hunched over and completely covered in shawls so that she isn't recognizable, appears before Kikushyo]*

KIKUSHYO. *[Kindly]* Old woman. How can I help you?

KIYOMI. Great master. The beauty of your paintings is known far and wide. I have come, a silly old woman, to ask a favor beyond my rights.

KIKUSHYO. What is it, old woman?

KIYOMI. *[She begins unwrapping a kimono]* Many years ago I danced in this kimono. She and I are both now old and tattered, and our dancing days are long behind us. I would like you to paint a picture of me in my kimono, before we are both gone forever.

KIKUSHYO. *[Looking at the kimono]* Silver birds. Kiyomi-san, is it you?

KIYOMI. How do you know my name, master?

KIKUSHYO. Do you remember, long, long, ago, you gave shelter to a young man on his way to the royal city? And that young man saw you dancing for the spirit of your True Love?

KIYOMI. You?

KIKUSHYO. Yes. That young man was I, Kikushyo! And now, at last, I can repay you for your kindness on that night. Your portrait will be the greatest work of my life.

NUSHI. And so Kikushyo painted Kiyomi's portrait, not as an old woman, but as the beautiful young lady he remembered, dancing with all her heart on that moonlit night so long ago. And when he had finished the painting, and he showed Kiyomi, she wept with joy. *[The painting can be simply a piece of translucent material. When KIYOMI holds it up, we see her through the material]*

KIYOMI. My heart dances to the music of your brush strokes, kind master. Thank you . . . Kikushyo-san.

NUSHI. Then Kiyomi said farewell and set out on the road back to her cottage. Kikushyo worried that she was too old to travel so far, so he quietly followed behind her to make certain that no harm would befall her. They walked for nearly two days, dotsu-dotsu-dotsu, until they arrived at the cottage in the forest. *(Music #11B)*

> *[Night. KIKUSHYO creeps up to the window and peers in. He sees KIYOMI look once more at the painting. Then she kneels before the picture of the Spirit. Silence. KIYOMI remains perfectly still. Finally, KIKUSHYO quietly enters the cottage]*

KIKUSHYO. *[Clearing his throat]* Kiyomi. It is I, Kikushyo. Once more I am a guest in your cottage. *[She doesn't move]* Kiyomi-san? ... Kiyomi? *[He approaches and places his hand on her shoulder]*

NUSHI. And then Kikushyo understood that Kiyomi had changed her world. He stepped away and knelt in the corner where he had tried in vain to sleep those many years ago. And then he was certain he could see the spirit of Kiyomi rise and join the spirit of her True Love.

Music #11C: KIYOMI'S DANCE reprise

> *[The young KIYOMI emerges from beneath the bundle of shawls, dressed in her special kimono. She approaches the SPIRIT in his special LIGHT. She veils her face with the translucent fabric, as he does, so they are mirror images. They begin to move with the fabric, as mirror images of one another. Soon the fabric flows freely in the breeze of their dance. They link hands and dance together]*

NUSHI. And as Kikushyo watched, they danced together, two spirits, two happy souls united in one True Love. They danced to the music of the wind, in the night, on the moonlight.

> *[LIGHTS slowly out on Kikushyo and Kiyomi, up more brightly on NUSHI and KIMBERLY-KAY, who is still looking at the spot where the lovers had danced a moment ago. Silence, broken finally by:]*

KIMBERLY-KAY. *[Troubled]* What does it mean?

NUSHI. It means nothing. And it means everything. It is only a story.

KIMBERLY-KAY. So it isn't really true, right?

NUSHI. Only your heart can tell you that, Kim-Kay. If the story made you feel something . . . then it has truth. *[NUSHI backs away from KIMBERLY-KAY, who is still focused on the spot where the lovers danced. When she turns to look at NUSHI, he is gone]*

KIMBERLY-KAY. Nushi! He's gone. I wanted to tell him . . . I do feel something—sad, but a warm kind of sad. I wish—I wish—No, I don't. Wishes are for fairy tales. And I'm a—I'm a—I've had enough of these dumb stories, and I'm tired of being stuck in the middle of Nowhere. Take me back to my bedroom. Please?

PART III

[Suddenly a male "BREEZE," laughing uproariously and throwing snow everywhere, blows busily across the stage and exits]

KIMBERLY-KAY. Hey! . . . I wonder who he was. Hello? *[KIMBERLY-KAY goes to the exit through which the "BREEZE" disappeared and calls after him, but he appears at one of the other entrances, still laughing, and again quickly crosses the stage and exits]* How rude! . . . Hey, buster! *[Again she shouts in the direction he just left, and again he appears at an unexpected place. He is in constant motion]*

BLUSTER. The name's Bluster, not Buster.

KIMBERLY-KAY. Will you hold still?!

BLUSTER. Can't! Gotta blow! *[He is about to exit again, but this time KIMBERLY-KAY manages to stop him]*

KIMBERLY-KAY. Now wait just a second, Bluster, or whatever your name is. Aren't you supposed to tell me my third story, so I can get out of this place?

BLUSTER. Well, yes, but— *[He tries to get around her to the exit, but she blocks his way]*

KIMBERLY-KAY. But what?

BLUSTER. It's just that I have a lot to do and a long way to go. See, I'm a north wind, and I have to blow a snowstorm from Germany down through Hungary to Italy before the sun comes up. Besides, I've heard about you, and I've got better things to do than waste a story on a sourpuss, so if you'll excuse me—

KIMBERLY-KAY. *[Not so bossy as before]* Wait. You're right, I am a sourpuss. And . . . and . . . and it's a terrible curse. *[Turning on the pathos]* Haven't you got a story that will cure me?

BLUSTER. Oh, you poor child. They didn't tell me you were cursed. Well, I suppose I do have time for a quick story.

KIMBERLY-KAY. Great! Is it a romantic story like the one Brisa told me, or a sad story like Nushi's?

BLUSTER. Well, I've been blowing around for a long time, so I've picked up lots of stories. But the one I like best . . . *[He begins to giggle in anticipation]*

KIMBERLY-KAY. What's so funny? *[BLUSTER starts to answer, then his laughter goes out of control. Suddenly he stops laughing and assumes a professorial demeanor]*

BLUSTER. Enough frivolity. Story-telling's a serious business. Now then, the story of "Quack, Quack, Stick to My Back." *[Music #12. He again bursts into peals of hysterical laughter, and just as quickly turns himself off]* Once upon a time . . . in a kingdom called Austro-slash-Hungaro-slash-Italo-hyphen-Beederburg, there lived two young people. One was a Princess named Anna, who had everything— *[SPECIAL up on ANNA]*

ANNA. —money, jewels, servants, fast horses.

BLUSTER. And the other was Janos the Peasant— *[SPECIAL up on JANOS (pronounced YAH-nos)]* —a poor, young man who had nothing. Well. Almost nothing. He did have a bad case of . . .

JANOS. *[Sheepishly]* Scalp disease. Heh heh. *[He ruffles his hair and confetti comes flying out in all directions]*

BLUSTER. But even though Janos the Peasant had nothing . . . except—

JANOS. —scalp disease— *[a few more bits of confetti]*

BLUSTER. —he was basically happy and enjoyed his simple life, tending his father's sheep. *[Several members of the ENSEMBLE voice a burst of SHEEP noise]* Princess Anna, on the other hand, even though she had everything—

ANNA. *[Bored]* —money, jewels, servants, fast horses—

BLUSTER. —was nothing but a sourpuss. She never laughed. She never even smiled. Nothing pleased her. She just frowned. *And* sighed. *And* snapped at people. *And*—

ANNA. *[Snapping]* All right, all right, they get the idea!

BLUSTER. See what I mean? Now Princess Anna's father— *[SPECIAL up on the KING. FANFARE with kazoos]*

KING. *[Striking a kingly pose]* —The King!—

BLUSTER. —hated to see his daughter so unhappy. So he sent out a decree that the first man who could make his daughter laugh would win her hand in marriage and inherit the kingdom of Austro-slash-Hungaro-slash-Italo-hyphen-Beederburg. Janos the Peasant went to his mother and said—

JANOS. Mama, Princess Anna's father— *[FANFARE]*

KING. —The King!—

JANOS. —has said that any man who can make the Princess laugh will win her hand in marriage. I believe I will try this challenge.

JANOS'S MOTHER. But Janny, the Princess is very beautiful, and princes and noblemen will come from all over the world to win her hand. How can you, an uneducated peasant boy, hope to compete with them? Besides, you have—

JANOS. —I know. Scalp disease. But what do I have to lose?

KING. Funny you should ask. My daughter—

ANNA. *[Malevolently]* —The Princess!—

KING. —in order to make the contest more interesting, has requested that whoever tries to make her laugh and fails will lose his head. You know how she is, heh heh. *[JANOS and his MOTHER look at each other, concerned]*

JANOS. Nevertheless, I will try to make the Princess laugh. But I must travel the countryside and find a funny thing.

BLUSTER. So Janos said good-bye to his mother—

JANOS'S MOTHER. Stay on the path, and don't talk to strangers!

BLUSTER. *[Music #13]* —and set out to find a funny thing by which to make the Princess laugh. Meanwhile, back at the Palace.

PRINCE ONE. Good day, sir, are you— *[FANFARE]*

KING. *[Striking his pose with less enthusiasm]* —The King, yes. Who are you and what do you want?

PRINCE ONE. I am Prince One, and I have come to win the hand of your daughter by making her laugh.

KING. *[Brightening]* Ah, yes, come in, my boy, come in. Prince One, you say, well, yes, and you look like a fine young man. If you can make my daughter laugh, you shall have her hand and inherit the kingdom of Austro-slash-Hungaro-slash-Italo-hyphen-Beederburg. But if you fail . . . *[Suddenly losing his geniality]* She'll have your head.

BLUSTER. And so Prince One was led to Princess Anna, and the citizens were notified that the first suitor had come to try his luck.

HAROLD THE HERALD. Hear ye, hear ye! Now appearing at the Palace, for one night only, that prince of comedians, the Funny Man himself—Prince One! *[Polite applause from the ENSEMBLE, who now become the Palace audience. PRINCE ONE acknowledges the ovation while glancing nervously at the EXECUTIONER, who stands silently by]*

PRINCE ONE. Thank you, thank you. It's always a pleasure to play the Palace, and you know, it's a special pleasure tonight because I'm here to entertain this lovely, lovely lady, the Princess. Thank you very much.

ANNA. Get on with it.

PRINCE ONE. You bet. All right, this one will kill you. What do you call an out-of-work court jester?

ENSEMBLE. What?

PRINCE ONE. Nobody's fool! *[ANNA remains stone-faced]*

KING. She didn't laugh.

PRINCE ONE. Well, I'm just getting warmed up. This next joke will—

KING. *[To the Executioner]* Take him away.

PRINCE ONE. *[As he is led off, his voice fading]* Wait, wait, uh, how many peasants does it take to light a candle? Three: one to hold the candle, one to— *[SOUND of blade hitting block]*

BLUSTER. And so the people went home, very disappointed that Prince One had not been able to make the Princess laugh. *[ENSEMBLE disperses. Music #14]*

BLUSTER. While in another part of the kingdom, Janos the Peasant continued his search for a funny thing. One day he came upon a poor woman, trudging along the road.

WOMAN ONE. Trudge. Trudge. Trudge.

JANOS. Good day, madam, and how are you today?

WOMAN ONE. Could be better. What are you so happy about?

JANOS. I'm happy because I'm going to find a way to make the Princess laugh so I can wed her and become the king of Austro-slash-Hungaro-slash-Italo-hyphen-Beederburg.

WOMAN ONE. *[Laughing robustly]* A king with scalp disease?! Don't be silly.

JANOS. I know, I know, it's hard to believe, but I'll do it, just the same.

WOMAN ONE. Ah, well, you've given *me* a good laugh, I'll say that much, but the Princess won't be so easy. Say, got anything to eat?

JANOS. Just these three loaves of bread, but they're all I have for my journey and— *[The WOMAN holds out her hand. JANOS thinks for a moment, then hands her one of the loaves. She tucks it into her coat and holds out her hand again. Reluctantly, JANOS gives her a second loaf. She tucks that one away, too, and holds out her hand again]* This is my last loaf. If I give it to you I'll have nothing for myself . . . But I can see that you're very poor and very hungry. Here, take it. I'll manage without.

WOMAN ONE. Thank you, child. And now, to repay you your good deed, I have a present for you. Take this little flute. It will come in handy. *[JANOS takes the flute, plays a merry phrase of music on it, (Music #15) and he and the WOMAN laugh. They shake hands and head off in opposite directions]*

BLUSTER. Meanwhile, back at the Palace. *[PRINCE TWO enters. He is played by the same actor who played Prince One]*

PRINCE TWO. *[To the King]* Are you the Princess who never laughs?

KING. What? No, of course not, I'm— *[FANFARE]* —The King! Who are you?

PRINCE TWO. My name is Prince Two. I've come to win Princess Anna's hand.

KING. Prince Two? Are you any relation to Prince One?

PRINCE TWO. He's my father's only son, but his mother was my brother's aunt's sister. So we're distantly related.

KING. *[Totally confused]* I see. Well, I hope you have better luck with my daughter than he did. *[PRINCE TWO hands a card to Harold. As HAROLD reads it, the ENSEMBLE again gathers around]*

HAROLD THE HERALD. Hear ye, hear ye! Now appearing at the Palace, the man who would be King, that master of the royal put-down, Prince Two! *[APPLAUSE]*

PRINCE TWO. Thank you, Harold. Great guy, Harold—talks like his undershirt is two sizes too small. And speaking of small, this kingdom? right?—it's the only kingdom I know whose name is longer than its main highway. I'm serious; they had to rent space in Italy just to put up their welcome sign. And our King! —nice guy, but a few florins short in the brains department, if you know what I mean: the other day I saw him trying to catch a butterfly in his hat. *[The KING takes off his crown and looks at it, confused. PRINCE TWO continues as though to a two-year-old]* It's a crown, Your Majesty: it has a big hole in it. *[Back to audience]* No, I love the guy, I really do, but his taste in clothes is for poopoo. I mean, really, Your Putridness, who designed your royal robes, the Jolly Green Giant?

KING. *[Motioning to the Executioner]* Not amusing.

PRINCE TWO. *[As EXECUTIONER takes him away]* But the funniest guy in the kingdom is this executioner, he's a scream, he is; he just kills me. I laugh my head off when I'm around this guy, I really do, and I hear he knocks 'em dead down at the— *[The PRINCE's routine fades away and ends altogether as we hear the SOUND of blade hitting block. The ENSEMBLE disperses, glumly]*

BLUSTER. So Prince Two had fared no better than his brother's aunt's sister's son, Prince One. The people of the kingdom began to wonder if the Princess could ever be made to laugh. Nevertheless, Janos the Peasant continued his search for a funny thing.

[JANOS, walking along, meets WOMAN TWO, played by the same actress who played Woman One]

JANOS. Good morning, madam, and how are you on this fine— Excuse me, but you look very familiar. Didn't I meet you a few days ago and you gave me this flute?

WOMAN TWO. No, that must have been my father's sister's mother's only son's only daughter, who lives on the other side of Austro-slash-Hungaro-slash-Italo-hyphen-Beederburg. But she doesn't look anything like me, so I don't know how you ever guessed. Got anything to eat?

JANOS. No, I'm sorry, I gave my only food to—to your father's sister's mother's only son's only daughter. She was *very* hungry. But I do have a little money left, three florins.

WOMAN TWO. Better than nothing. *[She holds out her hand]*

JANOS. Share and share alike, my mother always told me. Here you are, and may God be with you. *[He hands her a florin, then starts to carry on past her, but she grabs him and holds out her hand again]* Oh. Yes. Well. Have another, I insist. *[He hands her a second coin and she pockets it without letting go of his collar. She holds her hand out. He looks at the audience, shrugs, then gives her the third coin]*

WOMAN TWO. Your mother would be proud. And to repay you for your kindness, I have a present for you. *[From under her coat or dress, she pulls a large goose. It's a puppet that fits over the lower arm of whoever is holding the goose]* This is Gertrude. She's a goose. And if you play the flute given to you by my father's sister's mother's only son's only daughter, Gertrude will dance a gigue for you. Go ahead, play. *[He does, (Music #16) and the goose, manipulated by WOMAN TWO, dances a funny dance. JANOS is delighted]* One other thing. Now that Gertrude knows you are her master, if anyone else touches her, she will cry, "Quack, quack," and then right away you must say, "Stick to my back." Quack, quack?

JANOS. Stick to my back!

WOMAN TWO. That's the ticket!

BLUSTER. Janos was delighted by Gertrude, the dancing goose. He thanked the woman for her gift and bade her farewell. Meanwhile, back at the Palace . . . *[Another PRINCE, played by the same actor, approaches the King]*

PRINCE THREE. Greetings, Mr. King. I am—

KING. Don't tell me. Prince Three, right?

PRINCE THREE. No, actually my name is Prince Fred. But you can call me Prince Fred. And these are my friends, Binky and Skeeter. *[He holds up two hand puppets]* Say, Mr. King, has anyone made the Princess laugh yet?

KING. No, they've all lost their heads trying.

PRINCE THREE. *[Oblivious]* Oh, good, then we're not too late.

KING. Exactly how do you plan to make my daughter laugh? We've had jokers and impersonators and even one fellow who drew a moustache on my face with axle grease— *[SOUND of blade hitting block]* That's him now. So what do you plan to do to amuse the sourpu—I mean, the Princess?

PRINCE THREE. We're going to take off all our clothes, put potatoes in our ears, and ride at full speed off the edge of the nearest cliff while singing "Onward, Christian Soldiers" in three-part harmony. Shall I set up right here? *[A long pause while the KING stares at Prince Three. Then he turns to the Executioner]*

KING. Take them away.

PRINCE THREE. Come on, boys, we're going on a trip with Mr. Executioner. *[They exit. SOUND of a small blade on block. PRINCE THREE speaks from offstage:]* Binky! *[SOUND of another small blade on block]* Skeeter! *[SOUND of full-size blade on block]*

BLUSTER. So still no one could make the Princess laugh. The entire kingdom of Austro-slash-Hungaro-slash-Italo-hyphen-Beederburg fell into a deep despair— *[The ENSEMBLE falls into a deep despair]* — except for Janos the Peasant. For although he had nothing, except—

JANOS. —scalp disease. *And* a flute. *And* a dancing goose.

BLUSTER. —still, he was happy, because he felt sure that he could make the Princess laugh, if only he set his mind to it. As night fell— *[SOUND effect: night falling]* —he arrived at an inn. *[JANOS approaches the INNKEEPER]*

JANOS. Good evening, madam innkeeper. Do you have a room for the night, for my goose and I are very tired and we plan to appear before the King and the Princess tomorrow to try our fortune in hopes of making the Princess la—

INNKEEPER. How much money have you got?

JANOS. Well, none, actually—I gave my last florins to an old woman who—

INNKEEPER. —Go sleep with a garlic-breathing dragoon. I'll have no freeloaders in my inn.

BLUSTER. But the innkeeper's daughter saw Janos's goose and instantly wanted it for her own. She whispered to her mother to let Janos stay, for that night she planned to steal the goose.

INNKEEPER. *[To Janos]* You can sleep in the barn, behind the stacks of hay. But whatever sounds you may hear, do not peek out from behind the hay. Especially if it's quacking sounds. Do you understand?

JANOS. Yes, madam innkeeper, thank you. I'm sure I'll be very comfortable there.

BLUSTER. So Janos made a bed for himself behind the hay and soon fell asleep. But late that night he was awakened by a strange noise, like little girl's feet walking on dirty floorboards. Then he heard the rustling of hay and the unmistakable sound of someone being dishonest. And then, plain as day and twice as loud, he heard Gertrude's cry:

GERTRUDE. Quack, quack!

JANOS. *[Jumping up]* Stick to my back!

BLUSTER. And when Janos came out from behind the hay, he found the innkeeper's daughter with both of her hands stuck to Gertrude. She pulled and she pulled, but no matter how hard she pulled, she couldn't get her hands loose.

JANOS. Ha! That'll teach you not to try to steal a fellow's goose. Well, you'll just have to sleep in the barn with us then, won't you.

BLUSTER. The next morning Janos rose to find the innkeeper's daughter sleeping next to Gertrude, still stuck fast to the goose.

JANOS. Wake up, you sleepyheads. What do you say, Gertrude?

Shall we dance along to the Palace and see if we can make the Princess laugh?

GIRL. But what about me?

JANOS. You can dance, too, if you like. In any case, since you've gotten yourself stuck to Gertrude, you'll have to come along.

GIRL. But—

[JANOS takes out his flute and begins to play (Music #17). GERTRUDE begins to dance, with the GIRL dancing wildly behind her. The INNKEEPER enters, sweeping, then stares in astonishment at the dancing goose and her daughter stuck to it]

INNKEEPER. Here, now, what is the meaning of this tomfoolery? Guinevere, unhand that goose!

BLUSTER. But the girl could not let go.

INNKEEPER. Guinevere, did you hear what I said? How dare you disobey me! *[The INNKEEPER swats her daughter with the broom]*

GERTRUDE. Quack, quack!

JANOS. *[Enjoying this immensely]* Stick to my back!

BLUSTER. And the innkeeper's broom stuck to the girl's behind, and now the innkeeper joined their dance. Just then, the mayor of the town happened along.

MAYOR. Why, of all the—I've never seen such despicable behavior in my town. Let go of that girl and unhand that goose!

BLUSTER. But of course they couldn't. They only kept on dancing.

MAYOR. I'll soon put a stop to this. *[The MAYOR huffs over to them and wraps his arms around the Innkeeper's waist]*

GERTRUDE. Quack, quack!

JANOS. Stick to my back!

BLUSTER. And now the mayor, too, joined the dance, and they all danced their way down the road that led to the palace.

[They exit. LIGHTS up on the KING, disconsolate, and ANNA, glum as ever]

BLUSTER. Meanwhile—

ANNA and KING. —back at the Palace.

ANNA. Cheer up, Papa. So, no one made me laugh and won my hand in marriage. Look at the bright side: now you'll have me all to yourself.

KING. Oh, joy. *[JANOS enters, alone]*
JANOS. So this is the Palace! And you must be— *[FANFARE]*
KING. *[Snapping]* The King, yes! Who let you in here, peasant?
JANOS. I've come to try my luck at making the Princess laugh. I hope to win her hand and become the king of Austro-slash-Hungaro-slash-Italo-hyphen-Beederburg.
KING. You?! But you're just a peasant. And you have a nasty case of—
JANOS. Don't say it—
ANNA. —scalp disease! And you want to be king?! Now that's *almost* funny.
KING. It is? Yes, I suppose it is. Perhaps this boy has a chance after all. But tell us how you propose to make our daughter laugh. Do you have some other funny ailments?
JANOS. No, just the scalp. But I have this flute.
KING. A flute?
JANOS. And Gertrude.
ANNA. Gertrude?
JANOS. And Gertrude's friends.
KING. Well, that doesn't seem very promising, but carry on.
JANOS. Don't I get an audience?
KING. No, I'm afraid they stopped coming weeks ago. They just wait outside for the executions now. *[JANOS raises his flute to his mouth, then pauses]*
JANOS. Just exactly how many heads have you cut off since this contest started?
KING. Well, depending on how you count the Siamese prince, it was either 233 or 234. *[JANOS puts the flute back in his pocket]*
JANOS. I don't really want to be the king, anyway.
ANNA. Wait . . . Try. I have a funny feeling about you. I think you can make me laugh.
JANOS. You really think so?
ANNA. No. But if your head is chopped off at least you won't have to worry about your scalp disease any more.
JANOS. *[Brightening]* That's true. All right. I'll give it a try.

[He raises the flute to his lips and begins to play (Music #18). After a moment, GERTRUDE dances on. Stuck to her back is the GIRL. Stuck to the Girl is the Innkeeper's broom held by the

INNKEEPER; stuck to the Innkeeper is the MAYOR; stuck to the Mayor is an oar held by a SAILOR; stuck to the Sailor is a WENCH; stuck to the Wench is a MAN pinching her bottom; etc. The entire ENSEMBLE, with the exception of those actors playing Bluster, Janos, Anna, and the King, is stuck in a long chain behind the goose. The KING looks at his daughter. ANNA watches their short dance in utter astonishment, then shouts:]

ANNA. Stop!

[For a moment, everything comes to a standstill. Then, like an earthquake gathering momentum, the corners of ANNA's mouth quiver, her shoulders start to shake, her whole body begins to tremble, a tiny shimmering squeak begins to emit from her mouth and gradually turns into the most outlandish guffaw you've ever heard. Soon the entire ENSEMBLE is laughing wildly; and as they do, the dancing chain breaks apart, freeing GERTRUDE, who happens to land in Kimberly-Kay's lap. EVERYONE laughs long and hard, lots of different kinds of laughs, different pitches, different rhythms, a symphony of laughter. Finally, the LIGHTS dim to black. The LAUGHTER fades out until it is carried by only one voice, KIMBERLY-KAY's. When the LIGHTS come back up, KIMBERLY-KAY is Center Stage under her covers, still laughing hysterically. After a moment, her MOTHER comes in and watches her. Finally, KIMBERLY-KAY emerges from under the covers, sees her mother, and her laughter instantly ceases in astonishment]

KIMBERLY-KAY. Mother! What are you doing in Nowhere?

MOTHER. Nowhere? What in the world are you talking about, Kimberly-Kay?

KIMBERLY-KAY. And where did Bluster go? I wanted to thank him for—How did I get back to my bedroom?

MOTHER. Well for goodness' sake, you never left.

KIMBERLY-KAY. Yes, I did. The Wind of a Thousand Tales came and carried me off to Nowhere and then these three breezes named Brisa, Nushi, and Bluster told me three stories and said if I didn't like them the wind would die out forever, but Mom, I *did* like them, I really did, and—

MOTHER. Kimberly-Kay. An hour ago, you had no imagination whatsoever, and now I come in here and you tell me about magical winds and breezes with funny names. What has gotten into you? Now I'm telling you you've been up here all the time; I could hear you talking to yourself.

KIMBERLY-KAY. *[Crestfallen]* You mean . . . it *was* a dream after all. The whole thing?

MOTHER. It must have been, sweetie.

KIMBERLY-KAY. Then there weren't any stories. I just dreamed them up. I don't know how— *[She is interrupted by a muffled "QUACK, QUACK." After a moment of confusion, she dives under her covers and comes out again, holding—]* Gertrude! It wasn't a dream! It was real!

MOTHER. Where did that goose come from?

KIMBERLY-KAY. Well, now that's an interesting story, Mom.

Music #21: FINALE

KIMBERLY-KAY. *[Sings:]* Life is more than math and science;
    I guess I'm a little surprised.
    I like stories and make-believe;
    They've made me stretch my mind!
    Red and green, blue and gray;
    I knew my fate, I was a child of tomorrow.
    Other worlds, just as bright!
    Once upon a time I was a child of tomorrow.

KIMBERLY-KAY and MOTHER. I was (You were) so serious,
    Couldn't wait to grow up!
    Now I've (you've) learned a little,
    Even dreamed a little,
    Reached for something above.
    Just let go,
    And try some make-believe!

ENSEMBLE. Once upon a time lived a princess;
    Once upon a time was a fable told,
    'Bout a man and his son,
    And the daughter of Juan,
    And the beautiful dancer, Kiyomi.
    Stories of love, stories of courage,
    Journeys in darkness, travels in light;
    Humor and wisdom, music and mirth:
    This is the Wind of a Thousand Tales—

Part III

This is the Wind of a Thousand Tales.
Once upon a time, once upon a time.
[Whispered, echoing:]
—happily ever after...
—happily ever after...
—ever after...
—ever after...

[When the song is over, all exit except for an OLD WOMAN, whose voice we heard at the top of the show, and two small CHILDREN, who are climbing into bed]

OLD WOMAN. And they lived happily ever after. And that's the story of how your Gramma Kim-Kay went to Nowhere.

CHILD ONE. *[Earnestly]* But it isn't really true, is it, Gramma Kim-Kay?

CHILD TWO. All that stuff about Brisa—

CHILD ONE. —and Nushi—

CHILD TWO. —and Bluster—

CHILD ONE. —and Gertrude?

CHILD TWO. *[With certainty]* It never really happened to you.

OLD WOMAN. *[With a gentle laugh]* Did it happen? Maybe, maybe not. But is it true? *[Brief gust of wind]* Is it true?

[The THREE look at one another intently. The CHILDREN smile. LIGHTS fade to black]

CURTAIN

PRODUCTION NOTES

Properties

PART I
    Bird-puppet, sheet of newspaper, umbrella, etc.—fly across the stage
    Flashlight—Kimberly-Kay
    Book—Corazón
    Valentine—Girl
    Candle, writing materials—Carlos
    Black blindfold—Ensemble Member
    Bundle of letters—under Carlos's "bed"
    Wedding regalia for Corazón—Ensemble Members

PART II
    Japanese straw hat—Nushi
    Rice (may be mimed)—Villagers
    Coins (may be mimed)—Mother
    Candles—Kiyomi
    Food, chopsticks—Kiyomi
    Futon—Kiyomi
    Screen (translucent cloth may be used instead)
    Kimono with silver birds—Kiyomi
    Sheathed knife—Kiyomi
    Translucent material—Spirit
    Aging make-up—Ensemble Member (applied to Kikushyo and Kiyomi)
    Shawls—Kiyomi
    "Painting" (see p. 23 for description)—Kikushyo

PART III
    Confetti—in Janos's hair
    Optional kazoos—Ensemble Members
    3 loaves of bread—Janos
    Small flute—Woman One
    Business card—Prince Two
    3 florins (coins)—Janos
    Goose hand puppet—Woman Two
    2 hand puppets—Prince Three
    Broom—Innkeeper
    Oar—Sailor

Costumes

In the original production, all actors wore black "unit" costumes to which various costume elements were added to create the different characters. The only exceptions to this were Kimberly-Kay and Gramma Kim-Kay, who wore realistic costumes. Because 10 of the actors were playing a number of roles each, it was found that the simpler the costume, the better. All costume changes happened on stage, in full view of the audience.

Production Notes 39

Music and Sound Effects

The play may be presented as a musical or non-musical. The only essential song is Corazón's, and this one may be lip-synched using the Demonstration Tape available from the publisher, or an appropriate folk song may be substituted. The English translation of the lyrics:

> Song of my heart;
> Song of love,
> Song of peace,
> Song of happiness.
>
> Song of my heart;
> With happiness,
> Singing of love
> All my life.
>
> Fly, my heart,
> Like a white dove,
> Free of pain,
> Filled with pleasure,
> Fly! Fly!
> . . .
> And my love, near me,
> Would lift me to the blue sky.
> We join the stars
> And dance with the little angels;
> Fly! Fly!

Accompaniment Tape of the instrumental music, which can be used as background music, interludes, etc., if and as desired. A complete score including songs and incidental music may also be purchased from the publisher.

"Child of Tomorrow": In the world premiere at South Coast Repertory in 1988, Kimberly-Kay referred to herself as "a child of the eighties." To give the song timelessness, the words have been changed to "a child of tomorrow." Producers during the 1990's may want to substitute "a child of the nineties." After the turn of the century, phrases like "a child of this century" (2 syllables) or "a child of the future" may be appropriate. Incidentally, the appearance of Kim-Kay as a grandmother at the end of the play does not mean that the rest of the story took place years ago; rather the final scene is a flash-forward.

The non-instrumental sound effects, such as the whispering and murmuring of the wind, the Kabuki clackers, wolves, owls, monkeys, etc., were made by the actors.

The Set

The original set consisted of three platforms on an otherwise bare stage. Costume elements and props were stored beneath the platforms until needed. To create the sense of empty space for Nowhere, the whole set was covered in black astro turf. Ensemble members holding cloth served as screens, and an oversized, lightweight bedspread in a quilt pattern served as Kim-Kay's bed when it was spread over one of the platforms. This bedspread billowed very nicely and helped suggest the effect of the breezes when they "blew" Kim-Kay to Nowhere.

Floor Plan

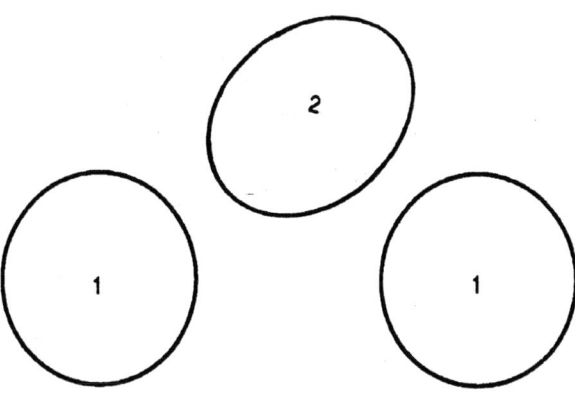

1—Round platforms
2—Ramped oval platform